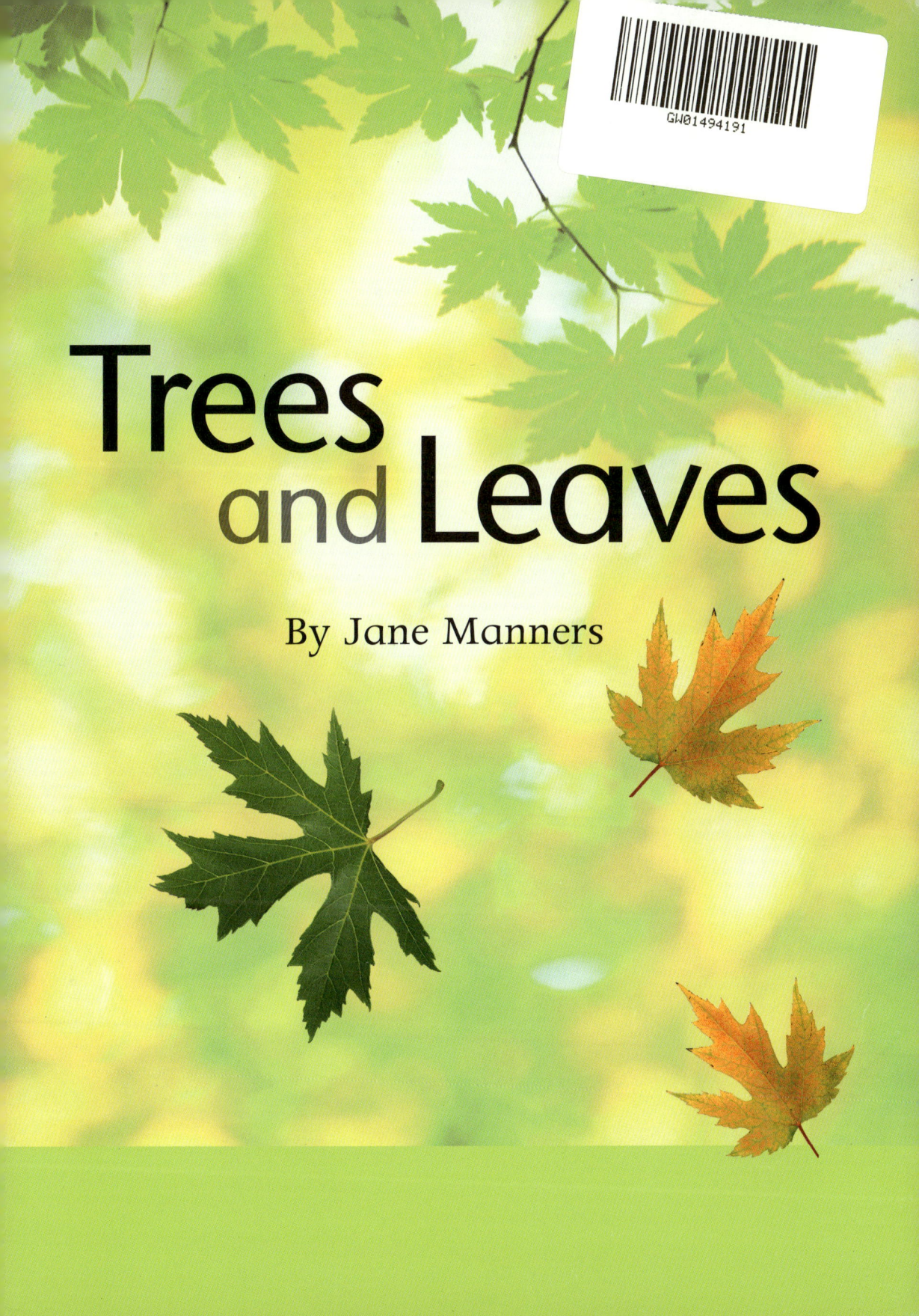

Trees and Leaves

By Jane Manners

Trees have leaves.

apple tree

maple tree

oak tree

eucalyptus tree

Different trees have different leaves.

apple   beech   birch

holly   cherry   lime

Some leaves are small.

plane

catalpa

Some leaves are large.

sweet chestnut

eucalyptus

tulip tree

ginkgo

Leaves have different shapes.

copper beech

maple

red oak

hickory

dogwood

Leaves have different colours.

There are many different types of trees and leaves.